NORTH AMERICAN ANIMALS

Cottontail Rabbits

by Christina Leighton

BELLWETHER MEDIA · MINNEAPOLIS, MN

BLASTOFF! READERS

3

Note to Librarians, Teachers, and Parents:

Blastoff! Readers are carefully developed by literacy experts and combine standards-based content with developmentally appropriate text.

Level 1 provides the most support through repetition of high-frequency words, light text, predictable sentence patterns, and strong visual support.

Level 2 offers early readers a bit more challenge through varied simple sentences, increased text load, and less repetition of high-frequency words.

Level 3 advances early-fluent readers toward fluency through increased text and concept load, less reliance on visuals, longer sentences, and more literary language.

Level 4 builds reading stamina by providing more text per page, increased use of punctuation, greater variation in sentence patterns, and increasingly challenging vocabulary.

Level 5 encourages children to move from "learning to read" to "reading to learn" by providing even more text, varied writing styles, and less familiar topics.

Whichever book is right for your reader, Blastoff! Readers are the perfect books to build confidence and encourage a love of reading that will last a lifetime!

This edition first published in 2017 by Bellwether Media, Inc.

No part of this publication may be reproduced in whole or in part without written permission of the publisher. For information regarding permission, write to Bellwether Media, Inc., Attention: Permissions Department, 5357 Penn Avenue South, Minneapolis, MN 55419.

Library of Congress Cataloging-in-Publication Data

Names: Leighton, Christina, author.
Title: Cottontail Rabbits / by Christina Leighton.
Other titles: Blastoff! Readers. 3, North American Animals.
Description: Minneapolis, MN : Bellwether Media, Inc., 2017. | Series:
   Blastoff! Readers. North American Animals | Audience: Ages 5-8. |
   Audience: K to grade 3. | Includes bibliographical references and index.
Identifiers: LCCN 2016033329 (print) | LCCN 2016042927 (ebook) | ISBN
   9781626175662 (hardcover : alk. paper) | ISBN 9781681032870 (ebook)
Subjects: LCSH: Cottontails–Juvenile literature.
Classification: LCC QL737.L32 L446 2017 (print) | LCC QL737.L32 (ebook) | DDC
   599.32/4–dc23
LC record available at https://lccn.loc.gov/2016033329

Editor: Betsy Rathburn   Designer: Brittany McIntosh

Table of Contents

Cottontail rabbits are **mammals** known for their fluffy, white tails. There are more than 15 types of these rabbits in North America.

eastern cottontail rabbit range = ▢

conservation status: least concern

Extinct

Extinct in the Wild

Critically Endangered

Endangered

Vulnerable

Near Threatened

Least Concern

The eastern cottontail rabbit is the most common. It can be found from southern Canada to Costa Rica!

Cottontail rabbits live in many different **habitats**. They are mostly found in grassy areas like farms and fields.

Some cottontails live in swamps or forests. Others even dash across deserts!

Cottontail rabbits come in different sizes. Females are usually larger than males.

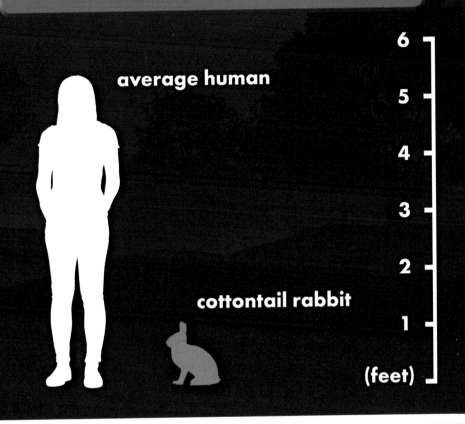

Size of a Cottontail Rabbit

average human

cottontail rabbit

6
5
4
3
2
1
(feet)

Cottontails are often between 16 and 19 inches (40 and 48 centimeters) long. They can weigh more than 3 pounds (1.4 kilograms).

Identify a Cottontail Rabbit

white tail

large ears

dark eyes

Cottontail rabbits have reddish brown or gray fur. Their eyes are big and dark.

Cottontails also have large ears. They can flatten them if they sense danger.

Avoiding Attacks

These rabbits must stay **alert**.
Many **predators** hunt them.

short-tailed weasels

golden eagles

bobcats

coyotes

red-tailed hawks

great horned owls

Raptors attack from above.
They are especially hard to escape.

Cottontail rabbits may freeze or sink low to the ground to avoid being seen.

They also quickly **zigzag** to safety. These rabbits can run about 18 miles (29 kilometers) per hour!

Cottontails mostly nibble on grass. These **herbivores** also eat fruits, clovers, and other plants.

On the Menu

alfalfa

bluegrass

clovers

strawberries

dandelions

wild rye

Some cottontails have a hard time finding food in winter. They eat tree bark and twigs to survive.

Fuzzy Kits

Female cottontail rabbits find **dens** or make ground nests to give birth. They usually do this three or four times a year. Their litters have up to 12 **kits**.

Baby Facts

Name for babies:	kits
Size of litter:	1 to 12 kits
Length of pregnancy:	25 to 28 days
Time spent with mom:	4 to 5 weeks

Kits are born blind and without fur. They **nurse** for about two weeks.

Soon, they can see and keep warm. The fuzzy kits leave the nest to explore!

Glossary

alert—quick to notice or act

dens—sheltered places

habitats—lands with certain types of plants, animals, and weather

herbivores—animals that only eat plants

kits—baby cottontail rabbits

mammals—warm-blooded animals that have backbones and feed their young milk

nurse—to drink mom's milk

predators—animals that hunt other animals for food

raptors—large birds that hunt other animals; raptors have excellent eyesight and powerful talons.

zigzag—to move in a path that has short, sharp turns

To Learn More

AT THE LIBRARY

Leaf, Christina. *Jackrabbits*. Minneapolis, Minn.: Bellwether Media, 2015.

Petrie, Kristin. *Cottontail Rabbits*. Minneapolis, Minn.: Abdo Publishing, 2015.

Robbins, Lynette. *Rabbits and Hares*. New York, N.Y.: PowerKids Press, 2012.

ON THE WEB

Learning more about cottontail rabbits is as easy as 1, 2, 3.

1. Go to www.factsurfer.com.

2. Enter "cottontail rabbits" into the search box.

3. Click the "Surf" button and you will see a list of related web sites.

With factsurfer.com, finding more information is just a click away.

Index

The images in this book are reproduced through the courtesy of: Arto Hakola, front cover; Don Johnston/ Age Fotostock, p. 4; Bruce MacQueen, pp. 6, 21; Maria Jeffs, pp. 7, 11; David Gowans/ Alamy Stock Photo, p. 8; Rob Hainer, p. 10 (top left); Yuval Helfman, p. 10 (top center, bottom); EverAmy14, pp. 10 (top right), 16; Wayne James, p. 12; Roberta Olenick/ Glow Images, p. 13 (top left); withGod, p. 13 (top right); Svetlana Foote, p. 13 (center left); Cynthia Kidwell, p. 13 (center right); Le Do, p. 13 (bottom left); mlorenz, p. 13 (bottom right); DaveMcDPhoto, p. 14; Rafael Ben-Ari/ Alamy Stock Photo, p. 15; Kazakov Maksim, p. 17 (top left); Pelevina Ksinia, p. 17 (top right); Scisetti Alfio, p. 17 (center left); topseller, p. 17 (center right); Quang Ho, p. 17 (bottom left); marilyn barbone, p. 17 (bottom right); Design Pics Inc/ Alamy Stock Photo, p. 18; Elena Elisseeva, p. 19; Age Fotostock/ Age Fotostock/ SuperStock, p. 20.